Skills Never Taught at School

Top Life Skills and How to Develop Them

by Creative Ink Press

Book "Skills Never Taught at School" by Creative Ink Press

Copyright © 2024

All rights reserved. No portion of this book may be reproduced in any form without permission from the publisher, except as permitted by global copyright law.

CONTENTS

Introduction 4

Mastering Financial Prudence: Creating and Tracking Your Budget 7

Embracing Mindfulness: Practical Steps for Daily Practice 12

Embarking on Your AI and Coding Journey: Practical Steps to Integrate AI into Daily Life 18

Enhancing Emotional Intelligence: Practical Steps for Active Listening and Empathy 24

Mastering Negotiation: Practical Steps for Thorough Preparation and Understanding Needs 31

Harnessing Self-Motivation: Setting Clear Goals and Celebrating Small Wins 39

Developing Social Skills: Engaging in Regular Social Activities and Practicing Communication 46

Mastering Self-Defense: Enroll in a Class to Learn Techniques and Build Confidence 54

Mastering Public Speaking: Practical Steps to Build Confidence and Skill 58

Mastering Conflict Resolution: Practical Strategies for Finding Common Ground 63

Mastering Leadership: Leading by Example to Inspire Others 68

Final Words.. 74

Introduction

Welcome to " Skills Never Taught at School," a practical guide designed to help you navigate various aspects of personal and professional development. In this book, we explore key skills that are fundamental to success in today's dynamic and interconnected world. Whether you are striving to excel in your career, build strong relationships, or enhance your personal well-being, mastering these skills can significantly impact your journey towards fulfillment and achievement.

The Importance of Life Skills

Life skills encompass a wide range of competencies that enable individuals to adapt, thrive, and lead fulfilling lives. These skills go beyond academic knowledge or technical expertise; they include abilities such as communication, emotional intelligence, problem-solving, and leadership. Developing these skills equips you with the tools to navigate challenges, make informed decisions, and effectively manage various aspects of your life.

Why This Book?

This book is crafted as a practical resource to empower you with actionable insights and strategies for mastering essential life skills. Each chapter focuses on a specific skill, providing a comprehensive exploration of its importance, practical techniques for development, and real-world applications. Whether you are a student, professional, entrepreneur, or someone eager to enhance their personal growth, you will find valuable guidance and exercises to help you on your journey.

How to Use This Book

Each chapter is structured to provide a deep dive into a specific life skill, offering:

- **Explanation and Importance:** An overview of why the skill matters and its relevance in various contexts.
- **Practical Strategies:** Step-by-step techniques and exercises to develop and strengthen the skill.
- **Real-World Applications:** Examples and scenarios to illustrate how the skill can be applied in everyday situations.
- **Challenges and Solutions:** Insights into common challenges associated with each skill and practical solutions to overcome them.
- **Reflection and Action:** Prompts for self-reflection and actionable steps to integrate the skill into your life.

What You Will Learn

By engaging with this book, you will:

- **Enhance Your Communication Skills:** Learn how to articulate ideas clearly, listen actively, and build rapport with others.
- **Develop Emotional Intelligence:** Understand and manage emotions effectively, fostering better relationships and decision-making.

- **Master Leadership and Conflict Resolution:** Lead teams with integrity, inspire others, and navigate conflicts constructively.
- **Improve Self-Management:** Set goals, manage time efficiently, and cultivate resilience in the face of challenges.
- **Expand Your Social and Self-Defense Skills:** Strengthen interpersonal relationships, practice effective negotiation, and ensure personal safety.

Mastering essential life skills is a continuous journey of learning, growth, and self-discovery. Whether you are just starting out on this path or seeking to refine your existing abilities, this book serves as a practical guide to empower you with the knowledge and tools needed to succeed in today's complex world. Each skill explored in these pages contributes to your personal and professional development, equipping you with the confidence and competence to navigate challenges and seize opportunities.

Join us on this transformative journey as we delve into the essential life skills that will empower you to thrive and achieve your fullest potential. Let's embark together on a path of growth, resilience, and mastery of life's essential skills.

Mastering Financial Prudence: Creating and Tracking Your Budget

Financial prudence is the cornerstone of financial stability and growth. It ensures that you are living within your means, saving for the future, and avoiding the pitfalls of debt. This chapter will guide you through the practical steps of creating a budget and tracking your expenses, helping you to take control of your finances and build a secure financial future.

Understanding the Importance of a Budget

A budget is a financial plan that outlines your expected income and expenses over a specific period, usually a month. It serves as a roadmap for your spending, helping you allocate your money effectively and avoid overspending. By creating a budget, you can:

1. **Gain Control Over Your Finances:** Knowing where your money goes helps you make informed decisions about your spending and saving.
2. **Avoid Debt:** A budget helps you live within your means and avoid relying on credit cards or loans for everyday expenses.
3. **Achieve Financial Goals:** Whether you're saving for a vacation, a down payment on a house, or retirement, a budget helps you allocate funds towards your goals.
4. **Reduce Stress:** Financial uncertainty can be a significant source of stress. A budget provides clarity and peace of mind.

Step-by-Step Guide to Creating a Budget

Creating a budget involves several key steps:

1. **Calculate Your Income:** Start by determining your total monthly income. Include all sources of income, such as salary, freelance work, rental income, and any other earnings. Use your net income (after taxes and deductions) to get an accurate picture of what you have to work with.
2. **List Your Expenses:** Next, make a comprehensive list of all your monthly expenses. Categorize them into fixed expenses (e.g., rent/mortgage, utilities, insurance) and variable expenses (e.g., groceries, entertainment, dining out). Don't forget to include occasional expenses like car maintenance or medical bills.
3. **Set Financial Goals:** Identify your short-term and long-term financial goals. Short-term goals might include saving for a vacation or building an emergency fund, while long-term goals could be buying a home or retirement. Assign a specific dollar amount to each goal and a timeline for achieving it.
4. **Allocate Funds:** With your income and expenses outlined, allocate funds to each expense category. Start with your fixed expenses, then distribute the remaining funds to variable expenses and your financial goals. Ensure your total expenses do not exceed your income.
5. **Adjust and Balance:** If your expenses exceed your income, you'll need to adjust your budget. Look for areas where you can cut back, such

as dining out less frequently or canceling unused subscriptions. The goal is to create a balanced budget where your income covers all expenses, and you still have money left for savings.

Tools for Budgeting

Several tools can help you create and maintain your budget:

1. **Spreadsheets:** Programs like Microsoft Excel or Google Sheets offer customizable templates for budgeting. They are flexible and allow you to tailor your budget to your specific needs.
2. **Budgeting Apps:** Apps like Mint, YNAB (You Need A Budget), and PocketGuard automate the budgeting process. They can link to your bank accounts, categorize transactions, and provide real-time updates on your spending.
3. **Pen and Paper:** For those who prefer a hands-on approach, a simple notebook can be an effective tool for budgeting. Manually recording your income and expenses can increase awareness and accountability.

Tracking Your Expenses

Creating a budget is only the first step; tracking your expenses is crucial to ensure you stick to it. Here's how to do it:

1. **Record Every Expense:** Consistently record every expense, no matter how small. This habit helps you stay aware of your spending patterns and identify areas for improvement.

2. **Use a Spending Journal:** A spending journal is a detailed log of your daily expenses. It can be a physical notebook or a digital document. Record the date, amount, and purpose of each expense.
3. **Review Bank Statements:** Regularly review your bank and credit card statements to ensure all transactions are accounted for. This practice helps you spot any discrepancies or unauthorized charges.
4. **Categorize Expenses:** Group your expenses into categories (e.g., groceries, utilities, entertainment) to see where your money is going. Most budgeting apps automate this process, but you can also do it manually in a spreadsheet or journal.
5. **Set Spending Limits:** Assign spending limits to each category based on your budget. Monitor your spending against these limits to avoid overspending.
6. **Adjust as Needed:** Life is unpredictable, and your budget may need adjustments. If you find you're consistently overspending in one category, reevaluate your budget and make necessary changes.

Practical Tips for Sticking to Your Budget

1. **Plan Your Meals:** Meal planning can save you money on groceries and reduce the temptation to dine out. Create a weekly menu and shop with a list to avoid impulse purchases.
2. **Automate Savings:** Set up automatic transfers to your savings account. Treat savings like any other fixed expense to ensure you consistently set money aside.

3. **Limit Credit Card Use:** Using cash or a debit card can help you stay within your budget. If you use a credit card, pay off the balance in full each month to avoid interest charges.
4. **Track Progress:** Regularly review your budget and track your progress towards your financial goals. Celebrate small victories to stay motivated.
5. **Be Realistic:** Set realistic spending limits and goals. An overly restrictive budget can lead to frustration and make it harder to stick to.
6. **Seek Support:** If you're struggling to manage your budget, seek support from a financial advisor or join a financial literacy group. Sharing experiences and tips with others can provide valuable insights and encouragement.

Financial prudence through budgeting and expense tracking is a vital skill for achieving financial stability and reaching your goals. By creating a budget, tracking your expenses, and making necessary adjustments, you can live within your means and build a secure financial future. Remember, the key to successful budgeting is consistency and awareness. Stay committed to your financial plan, and you'll be well on your way to mastering financial prudence.

Embracing Mindfulness: Practical Steps for Daily Practice

In today's fast-paced world, mindfulness offers a sanctuary of calm and clarity. By dedicating a few minutes each day to mindful breathing or meditation, you can significantly improve your mental well-being, reduce stress, and enhance your overall quality of life. This chapter will guide you through the practical steps to incorporate mindfulness into your daily routine, ensuring you reap its numerous benefits.

Understanding Mindfulness

Mindfulness is the practice of being fully present in the moment, aware of your thoughts, feelings, and sensations without judgment. It involves paying attention to the here and now rather than dwelling on the past or worrying about the future. Mindfulness can be cultivated through various techniques, with mindful breathing and meditation being two of the most effective methods.

Benefits of Mindfulness

Before diving into the practical steps, it's essential to understand the benefits of mindfulness:

1. **Reduces Stress:** Mindfulness helps calm the mind and body, reducing stress and anxiety.
2. **Improves Focus:** Regular practice enhances concentration and cognitive function.
3. **Enhances Emotional Regulation:** Mindfulness allows you to respond to situations with greater clarity and less emotional reactivity.

4. **Promotes Physical Health:** It can lower blood pressure, improve sleep, and boost the immune system.
5. **Fosters Self-Awareness:** Mindfulness helps you understand your thoughts and emotions better, leading to greater self-awareness and personal growth.

Getting Started with Mindful Breathing

Mindful breathing is a simple yet powerful way to start your mindfulness practice. Here's a step-by-step guide:

1. **Find a Quiet Space:** Choose a quiet place where you won't be disturbed. It could be a corner of your room, a park, or any place that feels calm and safe.
2. **Get Comfortable:** Sit in a comfortable position with your back straight but not rigid. You can sit on a chair, a cushion, or the floor. If sitting is uncomfortable, you can also lie down.
3. **Close Your Eyes:** Gently close your eyes to minimize distractions and focus inward.
4. **Focus on Your Breath:** Bring your attention to your breath. Notice the sensation of the air entering and leaving your nostrils, the rise and fall of your chest, or the feeling of your abdomen expanding and contracting.
5. **Breathe Naturally:** Let your breath flow naturally. There's no need to alter your breathing pattern; just observe it.
6. **Anchor Your Mind:** If your mind starts to wander (which it will), gently bring your focus back to your breath. You can use a mental note like "in" and "out" to help maintain focus.

7. **Practice for a Few Minutes:** Start with just a few minutes each day. As you become more comfortable, gradually increase the duration to 10, 15, or even 20 minutes.
8. **End with Gratitude:** When you're ready to end your session, take a moment to appreciate the time you've dedicated to your practice. Open your eyes slowly and re-engage with your surroundings.

Incorporating Meditation into Your Routine

Meditation is a deeper form of mindfulness that can enhance your practice. Here's how to get started with a basic meditation practice:

1. **Choose a Consistent Time:** Dedicate a specific time each day for meditation. Morning is often recommended as it sets a calm tone for the day, but any time that fits your schedule is fine.
2. **Create a Calm Environment:** Find a quiet, comfortable place free from distractions. You might want to use a meditation cushion or chair.
3. **Assume a Comfortable Position:** Sit with your spine straight and your hands resting on your knees or in your lap. Your eyes can be closed or slightly open, gazing downward.
4. **Focus on Your Breath:** Begin by taking a few deep breaths to center yourself. Then, let your breath return to its natural rhythm and focus your attention on the sensation of breathing.
5. **Use a Meditation Anchor:** An anchor can be your breath, a word (like "peace" or "calm"), a phrase (such as "I am at peace"), or a visual

image. Use this anchor to bring your focus back whenever your mind wanders.
6. **Observe Without Judgment:** Thoughts and distractions will arise. Instead of engaging with them, simply acknowledge their presence and gently return to your anchor.
7. **Set a Timer:** Start with a short duration, such as 5 or 10 minutes. Gradually increase the time as you become more comfortable with the practice.
8. **End Slowly:** When your timer goes off, take a few moments to remain still. Open your eyes slowly and take a few deep breaths before getting up.

Practical Tips for Maintaining Your Practice

1. **Start Small:** Begin with just a few minutes each day and gradually increase the duration. Consistency is more important than length at the beginning.
2. **Use Guided Meditations:** If you're new to mindfulness, guided meditations can be helpful. There are many apps and online resources available, such as Headspace, Calm, and Insight Timer.
3. **Create a Ritual:** Incorporate your practice into a daily ritual. It could be part of your morning routine, during your lunch break, or before bed.
4. **Be Patient:** Developing a mindfulness practice takes time and patience. Don't be discouraged by a wandering mind or initial discomfort.
5. **Join a Community:** Consider joining a mindfulness group or attending a meditation class. Sharing the experience with others can provide support and motivation.

6. **Keep a Journal:** Document your mindfulness journey. Write about your experiences, any challenges you face, and the benefits you notice. Reflecting on your progress can be encouraging.

Integrating Mindfulness into Daily Activities

Mindfulness doesn't have to be limited to formal practice sessions. You can integrate it into everyday activities:

1. **Mindful Eating:** Pay full attention to the experience of eating. Notice the colors, textures, and flavors of your food. Eat slowly and savor each bite.
2. **Mindful Walking:** Focus on the sensation of your feet touching the ground, the rhythm of your steps, and your surroundings. Walking can be a moving meditation.
3. **Mindful Listening:** When conversing with someone, give them your full attention. Listen without planning your response or getting distracted by other thoughts.
4. **Mindful Chores:** Turn routine tasks like washing dishes or folding laundry into mindfulness practices by paying attention to the sensations and movements involved.
5. **Mindful Technology Use:** Be aware of your interaction with technology. Set boundaries for screen time and practice being fully present when using digital devices.

Mindfulness is a powerful tool for enhancing your mental, emotional, and physical well-being. By dedicating a few minutes each day to mindful breathing or meditation, you can cultivate a sense of peace and presence that permeates all aspects of your life. Remember, the key to mindfulness is consistency and compassion towards yourself. Start small, be patient, and gradually build your practice. With time and dedication, mindfulness can become a transformative part of your daily routine.

Embarking on Your AI and Coding Journey: Practical Steps to Integrate AI into Daily Life

Artificial Intelligence (AI) and coding are revolutionizing the world around us, offering endless possibilities for innovation and efficiency. Whether you aim to improve your personal productivity, enhance your business, or simply stay ahead in a tech-driven world, learning AI and coding is a valuable investment. This chapter will provide a step-by-step guide to starting with tutorials, gradually incorporating AI into your daily life, and learning from successful entrepreneurs while continuously testing new ideas.

Understanding the Basics: Why AI and Coding?

Before diving into the practical steps, it's essential to understand why AI and coding are so impactful:

1. **Efficiency and Automation:** AI can automate routine tasks, saving time and reducing errors.
2. **Data Analysis:** AI can process and analyze vast amounts of data quickly, providing insights that can drive decision-making.
3. **Personalization:** AI can tailor experiences based on individual preferences and behaviors, enhancing user engagement.
4. **Innovation:** Coding skills enable you to create custom solutions, bringing your ideas to life and solving unique problems.

Step-by-Step Guide to Starting with AI and Coding

1. **Choose Your Programming Language:**
    - **Python:** Widely used for AI and machine learning due to its simplicity

and extensive libraries (e.g., TensorFlow, PyTorch).
- **JavaScript:** Useful for web development and integrating AI into web applications.
- **R:** Preferred for statistical analysis and data visualization.

2. **Begin with Online Tutorials:**
   - **Platforms:** Utilize free and paid resources such as Codecademy, Coursera, Udacity, and Khan Academy.
   - **Structure:** Follow a structured path that starts with the basics of the chosen language, progressing to more advanced topics.
   - **Hands-On Projects:** Engage in hands-on projects to apply what you've learned. Building simple applications, games, or data analysis projects can be very effective.

3. **Explore AI-Specific Courses:**
   - **Introductory Courses:** Look for beginner-friendly courses in AI and machine learning on platforms like Coursera (e.g., Andrew Ng's Machine Learning course) or edX.
   - **Specializations:** Consider specializations or nanodegrees that focus on specific aspects of AI, such as natural language processing or computer vision.

4. **Build a Foundation in Math and Statistics:**
   - **Key Topics:** Study linear algebra, calculus, probability, and statistics as these are crucial for understanding AI algorithms.

- **Resources:** Khan Academy and MIT OpenCourseWare offer excellent free resources.

Gradually Integrating AI into Your Daily Life

1. **Personal Projects:**
   - **Voice Assistants:** Create a simple voice assistant using Python and libraries like SpeechRecognition.
   - **Recommendation Systems:** Build a recommendation engine for movies or books using collaborative filtering techniques.
   - **Home Automation:** Use AI to control smart home devices, such as programming lights or thermostats to adjust based on your routines.
2. **Productivity Tools:**
   - **Task Automation:** Use AI tools like Zapier or IFTTT to automate repetitive tasks.
   - **Chatbots:** Implement a chatbot for customer service on your website using platforms like Dialogflow.
3. **Daily Learning and Practice:**
   - **AI News:** Stay updated with the latest trends and breakthroughs by following AI news portals, blogs, and podcasts.
   - **Coding Challenges:** Participate in coding challenges on platforms like LeetCode, HackerRank, and Codewars to sharpen your skills.
   - **GitHub:** Explore AI projects on GitHub. Contribute to open-source projects or start your own repository.

Learning from Successful Entrepreneurs

1. **Study Case Studies:**
   - **Innovative Companies:** Analyze how companies like Google, Amazon, and Tesla are leveraging AI. Understand their strategies, successes, and failures.
   - **AI Startups:** Learn from emerging AI startups. Many have blogs or case studies that detail their journey.
2. **Follow Influencers:**
   - **Industry Leaders:** Follow AI experts and successful entrepreneurs on social media platforms like Twitter and LinkedIn.
   - **Webinars and Conferences:** Attend webinars and conferences where these leaders speak. Engage in Q&A sessions and networking opportunities.
3. **Books and Biographies:**
   - **Recommended Reads:** Books like "Artificial Intelligence: A Guide for Thinking Humans" by Melanie Mitchell, "Superintelligence" by Nick Bostrom, and biographies of tech entrepreneurs like Elon Musk and Jeff Bezos.

Continuously Testing New Ideas

1. **Experimentation:**
   - **Hackathons:** Participate in hackathons to test new ideas in a collaborative and competitive environment.
   - **Side Projects:** Continuously work on side projects. These could be

enhancements to existing applications or entirely new concepts.
    - **Feedback Loop:** Gather feedback from users and iterate on your projects. Use data-driven insights to refine your AI models.
2. **Minimum Viable Product (MVP):**
    - **Lean Startup Methodology:** Develop a minimal version of your product to test your hypotheses with real users. Gather feedback and pivot as needed.
    - **Scalability:** Focus on creating scalable solutions. Ensure that your AI models can handle increasing amounts of data and users.
3. **Collaboration and Mentorship:**
    - **Peer Groups:** Join or form peer groups with other AI enthusiasts. Collaborate on projects and share knowledge.
    - **Mentors:** Seek out mentors in the AI and tech industry. Their guidance can be invaluable for your growth and learning.

Practical Tips for Success

1. **Consistency:** Dedicate regular time to learning and practicing AI and coding. Consistency is key to mastering these skills.
2. **Real-World Applications:** Focus on real-world problems and applications. This not only makes learning more interesting but also more impactful.
3. **Documentation:** Keep thorough documentation of your projects. This will help

you track your progress and can be a valuable resource for future reference.
4. **Networking:** Build a network of like-minded individuals. Attend meetups, join online forums, and participate in community events.

Embarking on the journey of AI and coding can be both challenging and rewarding. By starting with tutorials, gradually integrating AI into your daily life, learning from successful entrepreneurs, and continuously testing new ideas, you can harness the power of AI to drive innovation and efficiency in your personal and professional life. Remember, the key to success is persistence, curiosity, and a willingness to learn from both your successes and failures. With dedication and practice, you'll be well on your way to becoming proficient in AI and coding, opening up a world of possibilities.

Enhancing Emotional Intelligence: Practical Steps for Active Listening and Empathy

Emotional intelligence (EQ) is the ability to recognize, understand, and manage our emotions and those of others. High EQ is crucial for personal and professional success, as it enhances communication, relationships, and decision-making. This chapter will provide practical steps to enhance your EQ by practicing active listening and empathy in daily interactions.

Understanding Emotional Intelligence

Emotional intelligence consists of five key components:

1. **Self-awareness:** Recognizing and understanding your emotions.
2. **Self-regulation:** Managing your emotions healthily and constructively.
3. **Motivation:** Being driven to achieve for the sake of achievement.
4. **Empathy:** Recognizing and understanding the emotions of others.
5. **Social skills:** Managing relationships to move people in desired directions.

Active listening and empathy are fundamental to developing empathy and social skills, directly enhancing EQ.

Step-by-Step Guide to Practicing Active Listening

Active listening involves fully concentrating, understanding, responding, and remembering what is being said. Here's how to practice it:

1. **Be Present:**
   - **Focus:** Eliminate distractions. Put away your phone, turn off the TV, and give the speaker your full attention.
   - **Body Language:** Use open body language. Face the speaker, maintain eye contact, and nod to show you're engaged.
2. **Show Interest:**
   - **Verbal Encouragement:** Use phrases like "I see," "Go on," and "Tell me more" to encourage the speaker to continue.
   - **Non-Verbal Cues:** Nod, smile, and use facial expressions that show you're interested.
3. **Avoid Interrupting:**
   - **Wait Your Turn:** Let the speaker finish their thoughts before responding. Avoid interrupting or finishing their sentences.
   - **Pause Before Responding:** Take a moment to process what's been said before you respond.
4. **Reflect and Paraphrase:**
   - **Reflect:** Summarize what you've heard. For example, "So what you're saying is…" or "It sounds like you're feeling…"
   - **Paraphrase:** Restate the message in your own words to ensure understanding and show that you're actively listening.

5. **Ask Open-Ended Questions:**
    - **Encourage Dialogue:** Ask questions that require more than a yes or no answer, such as "How did that make you feel?" or "What do you think about this?"
6. **Provide Feedback:**
    - **Be Honest and Respectful:** Share your thoughts and feelings honestly but respectfully. Use "I" statements to express your perspective without blaming or criticizing.

Step-by-Step Guide to Practicing Empathy

Empathy is the ability to understand and share the feelings of another. Here's how to cultivate empathy in your interactions:

1. **Put Yourself in Their Shoes:**
    - **Perspective-Taking:** Try to see the situation from the other person's point of view. Ask yourself how you would feel if you were in their position.
    - **Imagine Their Experience:** Think about their background, experiences, and challenges that might be influencing their emotions.
2. **Acknowledge Their Feelings:**
    - **Validate Emotions:** Acknowledge and validate the other person's feelings. Use phrases like "I understand why you feel that way" or "It's okay to feel upset."
    - **Express Understanding:** Let them know you understand their emotions,

even if you don't agree with their perspective.
3. **Show Compassion:**
   - **Offer Support:** Offer help or support if appropriate. Sometimes, just being there and showing you care can make a significant difference.
   - **Be Kind:** Small acts of kindness, like a reassuring word or a gentle touch, can convey empathy and compassion.
4. **Listen Without Judgement:**
   - **Stay Neutral:** Avoid making judgments or assumptions about the other person's feelings or experiences.
   - **Accept Their Emotions:** Accept their emotions as valid and important, even if they differ from your own.
5. **Respond Appropriately:**
   - **Be Genuine:** Respond with genuine concern and interest. Avoid platitudes or dismissive comments.
   - **Offer Constructive Feedback:** When giving feedback, be constructive and supportive. Focus on solutions rather than criticism.

Incorporating Active Listening and Empathy into Daily Interactions

1. **In Personal Relationships:**
   - **Family and Friends:** Practice active listening and empathy with family and friends. Show genuine interest in their lives and validate their feelings.
   - **Conflict Resolution:** Use active listening and empathy to resolve

conflicts. Understand the other person's perspective and work towards a mutually beneficial solution.
2. **In the Workplace:**
   - **Team Collaboration:** Foster a collaborative environment by actively listening to your colleagues and understanding their viewpoints.
   - **Leadership:** As a leader, demonstrate empathy by acknowledging the challenges your team faces and offering support.
3. **In Customer Service:**
   - **Understanding Needs:** Listen actively to understand customers' needs and concerns. Show empathy by acknowledging their issues and working towards a resolution.
   - **Building Rapport:** Build rapport with customers by showing genuine interest in their feedback and experiences.
4. **In Community and Social Settings:**
   - **Volunteering:** Practice empathy by volunteering for causes that matter to you. Understand and support the experiences of those you're helping.
   - **Social Interactions:** Apply active listening and empathy in social interactions. Be present and engaged in conversations, showing respect and understanding for others' perspectives.

Learning from Role Models

1. **Study Examples:**

- **Public Figures:** Study how public figures with high EQ, such as Oprah Winfrey or Barack Obama, communicate and connect with others.
- **Mentors:** Identify mentors who demonstrate strong active listening and empathy skills. Observe and learn from their interactions.

2. **Read Books and Articles:**
   - **Recommended Reads:** Books like "Emotional Intelligence" by Daniel Goleman and "Nonviolent Communication" by Marshall B. Rosenberg provide valuable insights and techniques.
   - **Online Resources:** Read articles and blogs on emotional intelligence to continuously learn and improve your skills.

3. **Attend Workshops and Seminars:**
   - **Training Programs:** Attend workshops and seminars on emotional intelligence, active listening, and empathy.
   - **Role-Playing Exercises:** Participate in role-playing exercises to practice and refine your skills in a supportive environment.

Continuously Testing and Refining Your Skills

1. **Self-Reflection:**
   - **Regular Check-Ins:** Regularly reflect on your interactions. Consider what went well and what could be improved.
   - **Emotional Journal:** Keep a journal to track your emotional responses and

progress in practicing active listening and empathy.
2. **Seek Feedback:**
    o **Ask for Input:** Ask trusted friends, family, or colleagues for feedback on your listening and empathetic skills.
    o **Be Open to Criticism:** Be open to constructive criticism and use it to refine your approach.
3. **Practice Regularly:**
    o **Daily Practice:** Dedicate time each day to practice active listening and empathy in your interactions.
    o **Mindfulness:** Incorporate mindfulness practices to enhance your self-awareness and emotional regulation.
4. **Stay Committed:**
    o **Consistency:** Consistently apply active listening and empathy in your daily interactions. The more you practice, the more natural it will become.
    o **Persistence:** Be patient and persistent. Developing high emotional intelligence takes time and effort, but the rewards are well worth it.

Enhancing emotional intelligence through active listening and empathy is a transformative process that can significantly improve your personal and professional relationships. By being present, showing interest, avoiding judgment, and responding with compassion, you can develop deeper connections and foster a more understanding and supportive environment. Remember, the key to success is consistency, self-reflection, and a genuine commitment to improving your EQ. With dedication and practice, you can master the art of active listening and empathy, leading to a more fulfilling and emotionally intelligent life.

Mastering Negotiation: Practical Steps for Thorough Preparation and Understanding Needs

Negotiation is a critical skill in both personal and professional life. Whether you're closing a business deal, asking for a raise, or resolving a conflict, effective negotiation requires thorough preparation and a deep understanding of the needs and wants of all parties involved. This chapter will provide practical steps to master negotiation by preparing thoroughly and understanding the interests of all stakeholders.

Understanding the Basics of Negotiation

Negotiation is a dialogue between two or more parties aimed at reaching a mutually beneficial agreement. The key components of successful negotiation include:

1. **Preparation:** Gathering relevant information and planning your strategy.
2. **Understanding Interests:** Identifying the needs, wants, and concerns of all parties.
3. **Communication:** Clearly and effectively conveying your position while actively listening to others.
4. **Problem-Solving:** Finding creative solutions that address the interests of all parties.
5. **Agreement:** Reaching a consensus that is acceptable to everyone involved.

Step-by-Step Guide to Thorough Preparation

1. **Define Your Goals:**
    - **Identify Objectives:** Clearly define what you want to achieve from the

negotiation. Be specific about your goals.
- **Set Priorities:** Prioritize your objectives. Understand which ones are essential and which are negotiable.

2. **Research All Parties Involved:**
   - **Know Your Counterpart:** Gather information about the other party's background, interests, and negotiating style.
   - **Understand Their Needs:** Identify their primary needs, wants, and concerns. Consider their motivations and constraints.
   - **Analyze Past Negotiations:** If applicable, review previous interactions with the same party to identify patterns and preferences.

3. **Gather Relevant Information:**
   - **Market Research:** Understand the market conditions, industry standards, and competitive landscape related to the negotiation.
   - **Financial Data:** Collect relevant financial information, such as pricing, costs, and budgets.
   - **Legal and Regulatory Considerations:** Be aware of any legal or regulatory factors that might impact the negotiation.

4. **Develop Your Strategy:**
   - **BATNA (Best Alternative to a Negotiated Agreement):** Determine your best alternative if the negotiation fails. Knowing your BATNA gives you leverage and clarity.

- **WATNA (Worst Alternative to a Negotiated Agreement):** Understand the worst-case scenario to assess risks.
- **ZOPA (Zone of Possible Agreement):** Identify the range within which an agreement is possible, considering both your and the other party's interests.

5. **Plan Your Approach:**
   - **Opening Offer:** Decide on your initial offer or proposal. Make it ambitious but realistic.
   - **Concessions:** Plan potential concessions you're willing to make. Consider what you might ask for in return.
   - **Counteroffers:** Prepare responses to potential counteroffers. Think through various scenarios and outcomes.

Understanding the Needs and Wants of All Parties

1. **Active Listening:**
   - **Be Attentive:** Give your full attention to the other party when they speak. Avoid interrupting and show genuine interest.
   - **Ask Open-Ended Questions:** Encourage the other party to share their perspectives and concerns. Use questions like "Can you tell me more about…" or "How do you feel about…"
   - **Reflect and Paraphrase:** Summarize what you've heard to ensure understanding and show that you're listening. For example, "So what you're saying is…"
2. **Empathy:**

- **Put Yourself in Their Shoes:** Try to understand the situation from the other party's perspective. Consider their challenges, pressures, and motivations.
- **Validate Their Feelings:** Acknowledge their emotions and concerns. Use phrases like "I understand that this is important to you" or "I can see why you're concerned about…"

3. **Identifying Interests:**
   - **Distinguish Positions from Interests:** Focus on the underlying interests rather than the stated positions. Positions are what people say they want; interests are the reasons why they want it.
   - **Explore Mutual Gains:** Look for areas where both parties can benefit. Identify common interests that can lead to win-win solutions.

4. **Gather Feedback:**
   - **Seek Clarification:** If something is unclear, ask for clarification. Avoid making assumptions.
   - **Confirm Understanding:** Periodically summarize the discussion to ensure that both parties are on the same page.

Practical Steps During the Negotiation

1. **Set a Positive Tone:**
   - **Build Rapport:** Start with small talk to establish a positive connection. Show respect and appreciation for the other party's time and effort.

- **Stay Calm and Professional:** Maintain a calm and professional demeanor, even if the negotiation becomes tense.

2. **Communicate Effectively:**
   - **Be Clear and Concise:** Clearly articulate your points and proposals. Avoid jargon and ensure your message is understood.
   - **Use Persuasive Techniques:** Use logical arguments, data, and evidence to support your position. Appeal to common goals and interests.

3. **Stay Flexible:**
   - **Be Open to Alternatives:** Be willing to explore alternative solutions and compromise. Flexibility can lead to creative and mutually beneficial outcomes.
   - **Adapt to New Information:** If new information arises during the negotiation, be prepared to adjust your strategy and approach.

4. **Manage Emotions:**
   - **Stay Composed:** Keep your emotions in check and avoid reacting impulsively. If you feel overwhelmed, take a break to regroup.
   - **Acknowledge Emotions:** Recognize and acknowledge the other party's emotions. Show empathy and understanding.

5. **Focus on Problem-Solving:**
   - **Collaborate:** Work together to find solutions that address the interests of all parties. Use brainstorming techniques to generate ideas.

- **Address Objections:** Anticipate and address objections or concerns. Provide clear explanations and alternatives.

Reaching an Agreement

1. **Summarize Key Points:**
    - **Review Agreements:** Summarize the main points and agreements reached during the negotiation. Ensure both parties have a clear understanding.
    - **Clarify Details:** Clarify any remaining details or ambiguities. Confirm that both parties are satisfied with the terms.
2. **Document the Agreement:**
    - **Written Agreement:** Draft a written agreement that outlines the terms and conditions. Ensure it is clear, comprehensive, and legally binding.
    - **Sign the Agreement:** Have all parties review and sign the agreement. Keep copies for reference.
3. **Follow-Up:**
    - **Implement the Agreement:** Ensure that the agreed-upon terms are implemented as planned. Monitor progress and address any issues that arise.
    - **Maintain the Relationship:** Continue to nurture the relationship with the other party. Show appreciation and stay in touch to build trust and cooperation for future negotiations.

Practical Tips for Success

1. **Continuous Learning:**
   - **Read Books and Articles:** Study negotiation strategies and techniques. Books like "Getting to Yes" by Roger Fisher and William Ury and "Never Split the Difference" by Chris Voss offer valuable insights.
   - **Attend Workshops:** Participate in negotiation workshops and seminars to enhance your skills.
2. **Practice Regularly:**
   - **Role-Playing:** Practice negotiation scenarios with friends, colleagues, or mentors. Role-playing helps you refine your skills and build confidence.
   - **Real-World Application:** Apply your negotiation skills in everyday situations, such as negotiating prices or resolving conflicts.
3. **Seek Feedback:**
   - **Request Input:** Ask for feedback from others who have observed your negotiations. Use their input to identify areas for improvement.
   - **Self-Reflection:** Reflect on your negotiation experiences. Consider what worked well and what could be improved.
4. **Stay Patient and Persistent:**
   - **Be Patient:** Successful negotiation often takes time. Be patient and avoid rushing the process.
   - **Stay Persistent:** Don't be discouraged by setbacks. Learn from each

experience and continue to refine your skills.

Mastering negotiation requires thorough preparation and a deep understanding of the needs and wants of all parties involved. By defining your goals, researching all parties, developing a strategy, and practicing active listening and empathy, you can navigate negotiations effectively and reach mutually beneficial agreements. Remember, negotiation is not just about winning; it's about finding solutions that work for everyone. With dedication and practice, you can become a skilled negotiator, enhancing your personal and professional relationships and achieving your desired outcomes.

Harnessing Self-Motivation: Setting Clear Goals and Celebrating Small Wins

Self-motivation is the driving force that propels you toward achieving your goals and realizing your full potential. Unlike external motivation, which relies on outside influences, self-motivation comes from within, making it more sustainable and effective in the long run. In this chapter, we will explore practical steps to harness self-motivation by setting clear, achievable goals and celebrating small wins along the way.

Understanding Self-Motivation

Self-motivation is the ability to find reasons within yourself to pursue your goals and ambitions. It is fueled by personal desire, passion, and a sense of purpose. The key components of self-motivation include:

1. **Intrinsic Motivation:** Driven by internal rewards such as personal satisfaction, enjoyment, and a sense of accomplishment.
2. **Goal Setting:** Establishing clear, specific, and realistic goals that provide direction and purpose.
3. **Persistence:** The ability to stay committed and keep pushing forward, even in the face of challenges and setbacks.
4. **Self-Discipline:** Maintaining focus and self-control to consistently work toward your goals.

Step-by-Step Guide to Setting Clear, Achievable Goals

1. **Identify Your Vision:**

- **Reflect on Your Passions:** Think about what excites you and what you're passionate about. Your goals should align with your interests and values.
- **Visualize Your Future:** Picture where you want to be in the next 1, 5, or 10 years. This long-term vision will help guide your goal-setting process.

2. **Define Specific Goals:**
   - **Be Precise:** Instead of vague goals like "get fit," set specific goals such as "lose 10 pounds in 3 months" or "run a 5K in 8 weeks."
   - **Break Down Larger Goals:** Divide larger goals into smaller, manageable tasks. For instance, if your goal is to write a book, break it down into writing a certain number of pages or chapters each week.

3. **Ensure Goals Are Achievable:**
   - **Assess Your Capabilities:** Set goals that are challenging yet attainable. Consider your current skills, resources, and constraints.
   - **Set Realistic Deadlines:** Give yourself enough time to achieve your goals without feeling overwhelmed. Unrealistic deadlines can lead to frustration and burnout.

4. **Write Down Your Goals:**
   - **Create a Goal Journal:** Document your goals in a journal or planner. Writing them down makes them more tangible and helps you stay accountable.

- **Review Regularly:** Regularly review your goals to track your progress and make adjustments as needed.
5. **Create an Action Plan:**
    - **Outline Steps:** List the specific steps you need to take to achieve each goal. Include deadlines and milestones to keep yourself on track.
    - **Prioritize Tasks:** Identify the most important tasks that will have the biggest impact on achieving your goals. Focus on these first.

Celebrating Small Wins Along the Way

1. **Acknowledge Progress:**
    - **Track Milestones:** Break your goals into smaller milestones and track your progress. Celebrate each milestone achieved.
    - **Reflect on Achievements:** Take time to reflect on what you've accomplished so far. Recognize the effort and hard work you've put in.
2. **Reward Yourself:**
    - **Small Rewards:** Treat yourself to small rewards for achieving milestones. This could be something simple like a favorite snack, a movie night, or a day off.
    - **Meaningful Rewards:** Choose rewards that are meaningful and motivating to you. They should feel like a genuine treat for your efforts.
3. **Share Your Success:**

- **Tell Others:** Share your achievements with friends, family, or colleagues. Their encouragement and support can boost your motivation.
- **Celebrate Together:** If your goal involves a team effort, celebrate the successes together. Team celebrations foster a sense of camaraderie and shared accomplishment.

4. **Maintain a Positive Mindset:**
   - **Focus on Positives:** Concentrate on what you've achieved rather than what you haven't. This positive mindset will keep you motivated to continue.
   - **Learn from Setbacks:** Instead of dwelling on failures, view them as learning opportunities. Analyze what went wrong and how you can improve moving forward.

Practical Steps to Sustain Self-Motivation

1. **Visual Reminders:**
   - **Vision Boards:** Create a vision board with images, quotes, and reminders of your goals. Place it somewhere visible to keep your goals in sight.
   - **Post-It Notes:** Write motivational quotes or reminders on Post-It notes and place them around your workspace or home.
2. **Daily Habits:**
   - **Morning Routine:** Start your day with a routine that energizes and motivates you. This could include exercise, reading, or meditation.

- **Daily To-Do List:** Create a daily to-do list that aligns with your goals. Prioritize tasks that contribute to your long-term objectives.
3. **Stay Accountable:**
    - **Accountability Partner:** Find a friend or colleague who shares similar goals. Regularly check in with each other to stay accountable.
    - **Public Commitment:** Make a public commitment to your goals by sharing them on social media or with a group. The public declaration adds an extra layer of accountability.
4. **Continuous Learning:**
    - **Skill Development:** Continuously develop the skills and knowledge needed to achieve your goals. Attend workshops, take courses, and read books related to your objectives.
    - **Seek Inspiration:** Surround yourself with inspiration. Follow motivational speakers, read success stories, and join communities of like-minded individuals.
5. **Manage Stress:**
    - **Practice Mindfulness:** Incorporate mindfulness practices such as meditation or deep breathing to reduce stress and stay focused.
    - **Take Breaks:** Allow yourself regular breaks to rest and recharge. Overworking can lead to burnout and decreased motivation.

Learning from Role Models

1. **Study Successful Individuals:**
   - **Biographies and Interviews:** Read biographies and interviews of successful individuals who have achieved similar goals. Learn from their experiences and strategies.
   - **Mentors:** Identify mentors who can provide guidance and support. Their insights can help you stay motivated and navigate challenges.
2. **Analyze Their Techniques:**
   - **Goal Setting Strategies:** Study how successful individuals set and achieve their goals. Implement their techniques and adapt them to your own needs.
   - **Overcoming Obstacles:** Learn how they overcame obstacles and setbacks. Their resilience and problem-solving strategies can inspire you to keep going.

Practical Tips for Maintaining Long-Term Motivation

1. **Reevaluate Goals Periodically:**
   - **Assess Relevance:** Periodically reassess your goals to ensure they remain relevant and aligned with your values and priorities.
   - **Adjust as Needed:** Be flexible and willing to adjust your goals as circumstances change. Adaptability is key to maintaining motivation.
2. **Create a Supportive Environment:**
   - **Positive Influences:** Surround yourself with positive influences who support and

encourage your goals. Avoid negative influences that can undermine your motivation.
- **Organized Space:** Keep your workspace and living environment organized and conducive to productivity.
3. **Celebrate Major Achievements:**
    - **Big Celebrations:** When you achieve a major goal, celebrate in a significant way. This could be a special trip, a party, or a big reward.
    - **Reflect on Journey:** Take time to reflect on your journey and the growth you've experienced. Recognize the hard work and perseverance that led to your success.

Harnessing self-motivation through clear goal setting and celebrating small wins is a powerful strategy for achieving personal and professional success. By identifying your vision, setting specific and achievable goals, and rewarding yourself along the way, you can maintain the drive and determination needed to reach your objectives. Remember, self-motivation is a continuous process that requires persistence, discipline, and a positive mindset. With dedication and the practical steps outlined in this chapter, you can unlock your full potential and achieve your dreams.

Developing Social Skills: Engaging in Regular Social Activities and Practicing Communication

Social skills are essential for building relationships, advancing in your career, and navigating everyday interactions. Good social skills enhance your ability to connect with others, communicate effectively, and build a supportive network. This chapter will provide practical steps to develop your social skills by engaging in regular social activities and practicing communication.

Understanding Social Skills

Social skills are the abilities we use to interact and communicate with others effectively. Key components of social skills include:

1. **Verbal Communication:** The ability to express yourself clearly and effectively through spoken words.
2. **Non-Verbal Communication:** The use of body language, facial expressions, and gestures to convey messages.
3. **Active Listening:** Paying full attention to the speaker, understanding their message, and responding thoughtfully.
4. **Empathy:** Understanding and sharing the feelings of others.
5. **Conflict Resolution:** The ability to handle disagreements and conflicts constructively.
6. **Building Rapport:** Establishing a positive connection and mutual understanding with others.

Step-by-Step Guide to Engaging in Regular Social Activities

1. **Identify Opportunities:**
   - **Social Events:** Look for social events in your community, such as parties, gatherings, or networking events.
   - **Clubs and Groups:** Join clubs or groups that align with your interests, such as book clubs, sports teams, or hobby groups.
   - **Volunteer Work:** Participate in volunteer activities. This not only allows you to give back to the community but also to meet new people.
2. **Attend Regularly:**
   - **Commit to Attendance:** Make a commitment to attend social events and group meetings regularly. Consistency helps build relationships and improve social skills.
   - **Be Punctual:** Arrive on time to show respect for others' time and to make a positive impression.
3. **Engage Actively:**
   - **Participate Fully:** Engage actively in conversations and activities. Show interest and enthusiasm.
   - **Initiate Conversations:** Don't wait for others to approach you. Take the initiative to start conversations and introduce yourself.
4. **Step Out of Your Comfort Zone:**
   - **Try New Activities:** Experiment with new activities and social settings to

expand your comfort zone and meet diverse groups of people.
- **Attend Alone:** Occasionally attend events alone to challenge yourself and build confidence in social situations.

5. **Follow Up:**
    - **Stay in Touch:** Follow up with people you meet. Exchange contact information and reach out to maintain connections.
    - **Plan Future Activities:** Arrange to meet again for coffee, lunch, or another social activity to deepen the relationship.

Practicing Effective Communication

1. **Active Listening:**
    - **Focus on the Speaker:** Give the speaker your full attention. Avoid distractions and maintain eye contact.
    - **Show Interest:** Nod, smile, and use verbal affirmations like "I see," "Really?" or "Tell me more" to show that you're engaged.
    - **Reflect and Summarize:** Reflect back what the speaker has said to confirm understanding. Use phrases like "So, what you're saying is..." or "It sounds like you're feeling..."

2. **Clear and Concise Speaking:**
    - **Be Clear:** Speak clearly and at a moderate pace. Avoid mumbling or speaking too quickly.
    - **Use Simple Language:** Use simple and straightforward language to ensure your message is understood.

- **Stay on Topic:** Keep your conversation focused and avoid going off on tangents.
3. **Non-Verbal Communication:**
    - **Body Language:** Use open body language. Face the person you're speaking with, keep your arms uncrossed, and lean slightly forward.
    - **Facial Expressions:** Ensure your facial expressions match your words. Smile when appropriate and use expressions to convey empathy and interest.
    - **Gestures:** Use hand gestures to emphasize points, but avoid overdoing it, which can be distracting.
4. **Empathy:**
    - **Understand Feelings:** Try to understand and share the feelings of others. Ask yourself how you would feel in their situation.
    - **Validate Emotions:** Acknowledge and validate others' emotions. Use phrases like "I can see why you'd feel that way" or "That sounds challenging."
5. **Open-Ended Questions:**
    - **Encourage Dialogue:** Ask open-ended questions that require more than a yes or no answer. For example, "What do you think about…?" or "How did you feel when…?"
    - **Explore Topics:** Use open-ended questions to explore topics in more depth and keep the conversation flowing.
6. **Conflict Resolution:**

- **Stay Calm:** Remain calm and composed during conflicts. Avoid raising your voice or becoming defensive.
- **Listen to All Sides:** Listen to all perspectives before forming an opinion or responding.
- **Seek Solutions:** Focus on finding a mutually beneficial solution rather than winning the argument. Use phrases like "Let's find a way to resolve this" or "How can we make this work?"

Practical Steps to Enhance Social Skills

1. **Practice Regularly:**
   - **Daily Interactions:** Practice social skills in everyday interactions, such as with colleagues, neighbors, or service providers.
   - **Role-Playing:** Engage in role-playing exercises with friends or mentors to practice specific social scenarios.
2. **Seek Feedback:**
   - **Ask for Input:** Ask trusted friends, family, or colleagues for feedback on your social skills. Use their insights to identify areas for improvement.
   - **Self-Reflection:** Reflect on your social interactions. Consider what went well and what could be improved.
3. **Learn from Others:**
   - **Observe Role Models:** Observe and learn from people who excel in social situations. Note their body language, communication style, and ways of building rapport.

- **Study Social Skills:** Read books, articles, and watch videos on social skills and communication techniques.

4. **Stay Positive:**
   - **Maintain a Positive Attitude:** Approach social interactions with a positive attitude. Smile, be friendly, and show genuine interest in others.
   - **Handle Rejection Gracefully:** Not every social interaction will go smoothly. Accept rejection gracefully and view it as a learning opportunity.

5. **Improve Emotional Intelligence:**
   - **Self-Awareness:** Develop self-awareness to understand your emotions and how they affect your interactions.
   - **Self-Regulation:** Practice self-regulation to manage your emotions and respond appropriately in social situations.

Applying Social Skills in Different Settings

1. **In the Workplace:**
   - **Team Collaboration:** Use effective communication and active listening to collaborate with team members and build strong working relationships.
   - **Networking:** Attend professional events and networking opportunities to expand your professional network.
   - **Leadership:** As a leader, demonstrate strong social skills to inspire and motivate your team.

2. **In Personal Relationships:**

- **Family and Friends:** Use empathy and active listening to strengthen your relationships with family and friends.
- **Conflict Resolution:** Apply conflict resolution skills to handle disagreements constructively.

3. **In Social and Community Settings:**
    - **Community Involvement:** Participate in community events and activities to meet new people and build a sense of belonging.
    - **Volunteering:** Volunteer for causes you care about to connect with like-minded individuals.

Practical Tips for Long-Term Success

1. **Set Social Goals:**
    - **Specific Goals:** Set specific goals for improving your social skills, such as attending a certain number of events each month or initiating conversations with new people.
    - **Track Progress:** Keep track of your progress and celebrate your achievements along the way.
2. **Create a Supportive Environment:**
    - **Positive Influences:** Surround yourself with positive influences who encourage and support your efforts to improve your social skills.
    - **Practice Opportunities:** Seek out opportunities to practice your social skills regularly.
3. **Maintain a Growth Mindset:**

- **Embrace Challenges:** View challenges as opportunities to grow and improve your social skills.
- **Learn from Mistakes:** Learn from your mistakes and use them as stepping stones to better interactions.

4. **Stay Patient and Persistent:**
    - **Be Patient:** Developing strong social skills takes time and practice. Be patient with yourself and stay committed to your goals.
    - **Stay Persistent:** Don't be discouraged by setbacks. Keep practicing and refining your skills.

Developing social skills by engaging in regular social activities and practicing communication is essential for building meaningful relationships and navigating various social settings. By identifying opportunities, actively participating, and stepping out of your comfort zone, you can enhance your social interactions. Practicing active listening, clear communication, empathy, and conflict resolution will further improve your ability to connect with others. Remember, the key to success is consistent practice, seeking feedback, and maintaining a positive attitude. With dedication and effort, you can master social skills and enrich your personal and professional life.

Mastering Self-Defense: Enroll in a Class to Learn Techniques and Build Confidence

Self-defense is a crucial skill that empowers individuals to protect themselves in potentially dangerous situations. Beyond physical techniques, it encompasses awareness, prevention, and the confidence to handle adverse circumstances. Enrolling in a self-defense class is a practical step to learn these essential skills. This chapter will guide you through the process of finding the right self-defense class, what to expect, and how to build and maintain confidence through consistent practice.

Understanding the importance of self-defense is the first step. It is not merely about fighting back; it is about recognizing and avoiding danger, building self-assurance, and improving physical fitness. Self-defense classes teach practical skills that can be applied in real-world situations, enhancing your ability to stay safe. The confidence gained from knowing you can protect yourself can be transformative, impacting all areas of your life.

Finding the right self-defense class involves some research. Different styles of self-defense offer various benefits, so it's essential to choose one that aligns with your goals and interests. Krav Maga, for example, focuses on practical, real-world scenarios and is known for its efficiency in self-defense situations. Brazilian Jiu-Jitsu emphasizes ground fighting and submissions, making it ideal for close-quarters defense. Muay Thai and Taekwondo, with their emphasis on striking techniques, offer rigorous training that improves both defensive and offensive skills. Mixed Martial Arts (MMA) combines elements from various martial arts disciplines, providing a comprehensive self-defense toolkit.

When selecting a class, look for reputable instructors with proper training, experience, and certifications. A good instructor communicates well, makes students feel comfortable, and provides a supportive learning environment. Reading reviews and testimonials or seeking recommendations from friends or family can help you find a class that suits your needs. Consider the class format as well—whether you prefer group classes for their social interaction and varied practice partners, private lessons for personalized attention, or workshops and seminars for intensive, short-term learning.

In a self-defense class, you can expect a structured training program that begins with warm-up and conditioning exercises. Stretching and cardio activities prepare your body for the physical demands of training, while strength training builds the muscle necessary for effective self-defense techniques. As you progress, you will learn fundamental moves such as punches, kicks, and blocks, as well as defense strategies against common attacks like grabs, chokes, and strikes. Instructors often simulate real-world scenarios to help you apply these techniques in practical situations.

Active participation in drills and sparring sessions is crucial. Working with partners allows you to practice techniques and improve your timing and accuracy. Controlled sparring, where you engage in light, supervised combat, helps you apply what you've learned in a simulated environment, building both skill and confidence.

Building confidence through self-defense training involves consistent practice and positive reinforcement. Regular attendance at classes reinforces techniques and builds proficiency. Practicing moves at home further sharpens your skills and improves muscle memory. The encouragement and support from instructors and classmates boost your morale and self-assurance, creating a positive feedback loop that enhances your confidence.

Maintaining physical fitness is also vital. Incorporating a regular exercise routine that includes strength training and cardio helps you stay in peak condition, ready to defend yourself if necessary. A balanced diet fuels your body, enhancing your performance in training sessions and everyday activities.

Mental preparedness is as important as physical readiness. Awareness training teaches you to stay alert and recognize potential threats, helping you avoid dangerous situations before they escalate. Managing stress through techniques such as meditation or deep breathing can help you remain calm and composed under pressure, improving your ability to respond effectively in a crisis.

Continual learning is essential for long-term success in self-defense. As you become comfortable with the basics, consider enrolling in advanced classes to learn more complex techniques and strategies. Attending additional workshops and seminars keeps you updated on new developments in self-defense and helps you refine your skills.

In conclusion, enrolling in a self-defense class is a proactive step towards personal safety and empowerment. By researching and selecting the right class, actively participating in training, and maintaining a routine of regular practice and physical fitness, you can build the skills and confidence needed to protect yourself. Self-defense is not just about physical techniques but also about mental preparedness and awareness. With dedication and practice, you can master self-defense and feel secure in your ability to handle various situations.

Mastering Public Speaking: Practical Steps to Build Confidence and Skill

Public speaking is a skill that can transform your ability to communicate effectively and confidently in various settings, from professional presentations to social engagements. By starting with small groups and gradually increasing your audience size, you can develop the necessary skills to engage and inspire others. This chapter explores practical strategies and steps to help you become a proficient public speaker.

Understanding the Importance of Public Speaking

Public speaking is not just about delivering a message; it's about connecting with your audience, conveying ideas clearly, and leaving a lasting impact. Effective public speakers have the power to influence, persuade, and motivate others, making it a valuable skill in both personal and professional contexts.

Practical Steps to Build Your Public Speaking Skills

1. Self-Preparation: Before you speak publicly, thorough preparation is essential:

- **Know Your Material:** Research your topic thoroughly and gather relevant information.
- **Outline Your Speech:** Structure your content with a clear introduction, main points, and a compelling conclusion.
- **Practice Your Delivery:** Write a script if necessary, but focus on speaking naturally and confidently.

2. Practice in Front of a Mirror:

- **Observing Your Body Language:** Use a mirror to assess your posture, gestures, and facial expressions.
- **Refine Your Delivery:** Work on your tone, pace, and volume to enhance your delivery style.

3. Record and Review:

- **Use Technology:** Record yourself speaking using a camera or smartphone.
- **Evaluate Your Performance:** Review the recording to identify areas for improvement, such as clarity, fluency, and presence.

4. Start with Small Groups:

- **Family and Friends:** Begin by practicing with a supportive audience who can provide constructive feedback.
- **Join Speaking Clubs:** Consider joining organizations like Toastmasters to practice speaking in a structured and supportive environment.

5. Gradually Increase Audience Size:

- **Classroom Settings:** Volunteer to present in educational settings or workshops.
- **Workplace Presentations:** Offer to lead meetings or deliver presentations at work to gain confidence with larger groups.

6. Seek Feedback:

- **Request Input:** Ask for honest feedback from peers, mentors, or instructors after each practice session or presentation.
- **Reflect and Improve:** Use feedback to refine your skills and address areas needing improvement, such as clarity, organization, or engagement.

7. Develop Your Speaking Style:

- **Find Your Voice:** Identify your unique strengths as a speaker, whether it's storytelling, humor, or a calm demeanor.
- **Stay Authentic:** Be yourself; authenticity resonates with audiences more than a forced or unnatural style.

Overcoming Common Challenges in Public Speaking

1. Managing Fear and Anxiety:

- **Acknowledge Your Nerves:** Understand that it's normal to feel nervous before speaking.
- **Practice Relaxation Techniques:** Use deep breathing, visualization, or mindfulness to calm your nerves before speaking.

2. Engaging Your Audience:

- **Know Your Audience:** Tailor your message to their interests, needs, and knowledge level.
- **Maintain Eye Contact:** Connect with your audience by making eye contact to build trust and engagement.

3. Handling Mistakes:

- **Stay Calm:** If you make a mistake, pause, take a breath, and continue without drawing undue attention to the error.
- **Adapt and Adjust:** Be flexible and adapt your presentation as needed to maintain momentum and audience interest.

4. Maintaining Audience Attention:

- **Vary Your Delivery:** Use a mix of tone, pace, and volume to keep your audience engaged.
- **Use Visual Aids:** Incorporate slides, props, or videos to illustrate key points and maintain interest.

Practical Tips for Effective Public Speaking

1. **Preparation:**
   - **Research Thoroughly:** Understand your topic and gather credible information.
   - **Organize Your Content:** Create a clear and logical structure for your speech or presentation.
   - **Rehearse:** Practice multiple times to refine your delivery and ensure smooth transitions.
2. **Delivery:**
   - **Be Clear and Concise:** Use simple language and avoid jargon to ensure clarity.
   - **Use Gestures:** Employ natural gestures to emphasize key points and enhance your non-verbal communication.
   - **Maintain Eye Contact:** Engage your audience by looking at different

individuals throughout your presentation.
3. **Visual Aids:**
    - **Keep Slides Simple:** Use bullet points, images, or charts sparingly to support your message without overwhelming your audience.
    - **Practice with Visual Aids:** Familiarize yourself with any slides or materials beforehand to ensure seamless integration into your presentation.

Mastering public speaking involves consistent practice, self-reflection, and a willingness to step outside your comfort zone. By starting with small groups and gradually increasing your audience size, you can build confidence, refine your skills, and effectively communicate your message to any audience. With dedication and perseverance, you can become a confident and influential public speaker, capable of making a positive impact in various aspects of your life.

Mastering Conflict Resolution: Practical Strategies for Finding Common Ground

Conflict is an inevitable part of life, whether in personal relationships, workplaces, or communities. How we manage and resolve conflict can significantly impact our well-being and relationships. This chapter delves into practical strategies for mastering conflict resolution by emphasizing the importance of finding common ground and understanding perspectives.

Understanding Conflict Resolution

Conflict resolution is the process of addressing and resolving disputes or disagreements between individuals or groups. It involves seeking mutually acceptable solutions that satisfy everyone involved, thereby fostering constructive relationships and maintaining harmony.

Practical Strategies for Conflict Resolution

Conflict resolution involves several key steps and strategies to effectively manage and resolve disputes. Here are practical approaches to navigate conflicts and reach positive outcomes:

1. **Maintaining Calm and Objectivity:**

   - **Stay Calm:** Emotions can escalate conflicts. Maintain composure and approach the situation with a calm demeanor.
   - **Be Objective:** Focus on facts rather than assumptions or personal biases.

2. **Active Listening:**

- **Listen Actively:** Pay attention to what the other person is saying without interrupting.
- **Show Empathy:** Demonstrate understanding of their feelings and perspective.

3. **Identifying Core Issues:**

- **Clarify Concerns:** Encourage open dialogue to identify the underlying causes of the conflict.
- **Focus on Interests:** Determine the needs and interests of each party involved.

4. **Seeking Common Ground:**

- **Find Shared Interests:** Identify areas of agreement or common goals that both parties can work towards.
- **Explore Options Together:** Brainstorm solutions that address the concerns of all parties involved.

5. **Communicating Effectively:**

- **Use "I" Statements:** Express thoughts and feelings using "I" statements to avoid accusatory language.
- **Be Clear and Respectful:** Articulate your points clearly while maintaining respect for the other person.

6. **Negotiation and Compromise:**

- **Be Open to Compromise:** Understand that achieving a resolution may require both parties to make concessions.

- **Focus on Win-Win Solutions:** Aim for outcomes that benefit everyone involved.

7. **Seeking Mediation if Needed:**

    - **Involve a Third Party:** Consider mediation or arbitration by a neutral third party to facilitate discussions and find common ground.
    - **Professional Assistance:** Seek guidance from conflict resolution professionals or counselors for complex disputes.

8. **Reflecting and Learning:**

    - **Review and Reflect:** After resolving a conflict, evaluate what worked well and areas for improvement.
    - **Continuous Improvement:** Learn from each conflict resolution experience to enhance your skills and approaches.

Practical Application of Conflict Resolution Strategies

Example Scenario: Imagine a workplace scenario where two colleagues have conflicting views on how to approach a project. One colleague prefers a structured approach with detailed planning, while the other favors a more flexible, creative approach.

Step-by-Step Approach:

1. **Initiate Dialogue:** Start by inviting both colleagues to discuss their perspectives in a neutral setting.
2. **Active Listening:** Encourage each colleague to express their viewpoints without interruption.

3. **Identify Common Goals:** Explore shared objectives, such as project success and team collaboration.
4. **Brainstorm Solutions:** Collaborate to generate ideas that incorporate elements of both approaches.
5. **Negotiate and Compromise:** Reach a consensus by compromising on aspects of the project plan that accommodate both preferences.
6. **Agree on Implementation:** Finalize a mutually agreeable plan and agree on how to implement it effectively.

Overcoming Challenges in Conflict Resolution

1. **Emotional Responses:**

   - **Manage Emotions:** Practice emotional regulation techniques such as deep breathing or taking a break to regain composure.
   - **Focus on Solutions:** Redirect discussions towards finding solutions rather than dwelling on emotions.

2. **Power Imbalances:**

   - **Acknowledge Power Dynamics:** Address any perceived or actual power imbalances respectfully.
   - **Facilitate Fair Discussions:** Ensure all parties have equal opportunity to voice their concerns and contribute to the resolution process.

3. **Cultural and Personal Differences:**

- **Respect Diversity:** Appreciate cultural differences and diverse perspectives.
- **Build Cultural Competence:** Educate yourself on cultural norms and practices to navigate conflicts sensitively.

Mastering conflict resolution requires patience, empathy, and effective communication skills. By adopting practical strategies such as active listening, seeking common ground, and negotiating with a focus on mutual benefit, you can resolve conflicts constructively and strengthen relationships. Conflict, when managed well, presents an opportunity for growth and improved understanding among individuals or groups. With commitment to learning and applying conflict resolution techniques, you can navigate conflicts effectively and contribute to a more harmonious and productive environment in any setting.

Mastering Leadership: Leading by Example to Inspire Others

Leadership is not just about holding a position of authority; it's about inspiring and guiding others to achieve common goals. Effective leaders lead by example, demonstrating integrity, empathy, and vision through their actions and decisions. This chapter explores practical strategies for mastering leadership by leading through example and inspiring others in various contexts.

Understanding Leadership

Leadership is the ability to influence and motivate others to work towards a shared vision or goal. It involves making decisions, guiding teams, and fostering an environment of trust and collaboration. Effective leadership is characterized by qualities such as:

- **Vision:** Setting clear goals and inspiring others with a compelling vision for the future.
- **Integrity:** Acting with honesty, fairness, and ethical behavior in all situations.
- **Empathy:** Understanding and considering the perspectives and feelings of others.
- **Communication:** Articulating ideas clearly and listening actively to others.
- **Decision-Making:** Making sound decisions based on thoughtful analysis and consideration of diverse viewpoints.

Practical Strategies for Leading by Example

Leading by example means embodying the values and behaviors you wish to see in others. It involves demonstrating leadership qualities consistently and authentically. Here are practical strategies to cultivate and demonstrate effective leadership:

1. **Clarify Your Values and Vision:**

    - **Define Your Purpose:** Identify your core values and principles that guide your decisions and actions.
    - **Set Clear Goals:** Establish specific, achievable goals that align with your vision for yourself and your team.

2. **Act with Integrity:**

    - **Be Honest and Transparent:** Communicate openly and honestly with your team, even when delivering difficult messages.
    - **Demonstrate Ethical Behavior:** Uphold ethical standards and hold yourself accountable for your actions.

3. **Develop Self-Awareness:**

    - **Reflect on Your Strengths and Weaknesses:** Understand your strengths and areas for improvement as a leader.
    - **Seek Feedback:** Solicit feedback from peers, mentors, or team members to gain insights into your leadership style.

4. **Build Trust and Respect:**

- **Build Relationships:** Invest time in building positive relationships with your team members based on trust and mutual respect.
- **Delegate Responsibility:** Empower others by delegating tasks and trusting them to make decisions.

5. **Communicate Effectively:**

- **Articulate Your Vision:** Clearly communicate your goals and vision to inspire and align your team.
- **Listen Actively:** Practice active listening to understand the perspectives and concerns of your team members.

6. **Lead with Empathy:**

- **Understand Others' Perspectives:** Consider the feelings and viewpoints of others when making decisions.
- **Support Your Team:** Offer support and encouragement to team members, especially during challenging times.

7. **Make Decisions Thoughtfully:**

- **Gather Information:** Collect relevant information and seek input from stakeholders before making decisions.
- **Consider Impact:** Assess the potential impact of your decisions on individuals and the organization as a whole.

8. **Continuously Improve and Adapt:**

- **Embrace Learning:** Stay curious and seek opportunities for personal and professional growth.
- **Adapt to Change:** Be flexible and adaptable in response to changes in your environment or industry.

Practical Application of Leadership Principles

Example Scenario: Imagine you are leading a team tasked with launching a new product in a competitive market. As a leader, you want to inspire your team to work collaboratively towards achieving success.

Step-by-Step Approach:

1. **Articulate Your Vision:** Clearly communicate the vision for the product launch and the goals you aim to achieve.
2. **Lead by Example:** Demonstrate dedication and hard work by actively participating in planning and execution tasks.
3. **Encourage Collaboration:** Foster a collaborative environment where team members contribute ideas and work together towards common objectives.
4. **Provide Support:** Offer guidance, resources, and encouragement to team members to help them overcome challenges.
5. **Celebrate Success:** Recognize and celebrate achievements, both individual and team, to boost morale and motivation.

Overcoming Challenges in Leadership

1. **Handling Resistance:**

- **Listen and Understand:** Address concerns and objections with empathy and openness.
- **Engage in Dialogue:** Foster open communication to build consensus and overcome resistance.

2. **Managing Pressure:**

- **Prioritize and Delegate:** Manage workload by prioritizing tasks and delegating responsibilities effectively.
- **Seek Support:** Lean on your team and seek advice from mentors or peers during challenging times.

3. **Inspiring Innovation:**

- **Encourage Creativity:** Create a culture that values innovation and encourages team members to explore new ideas.
- **Reward Innovation:** Recognize and reward innovative thinking and initiatives that contribute to organizational success.

Mastering leadership involves a commitment to personal growth, continuous learning, and leading by example. By cultivating qualities such as integrity, empathy, and effective communication, you can inspire others to perform at their best and achieve shared goals. Leadership is not about having all the answers but about empowering others and fostering a collaborative environment where everyone can contribute and thrive. With dedication and practice, you can become a confident and effective leader capable of making a positive impact in any organization or community.

Final Words

Congratulations on completing your journey through the book. As you reflect on the valuable insights and practical strategies presented in this book, I encourage you to take a moment to consider the profound impact these skills can have on your life.

Throughout these chapters, you've explored key facets of personal and professional development, from communication and emotional intelligence to leadership, conflict resolution, and beyond. Each skill serves as a pillar that supports your growth, resilience, and ability to navigate life's challenges with confidence and clarity.

Embracing Lifelong Learning

Remember, mastering life skills is not merely about acquiring knowledge but embracing a mindset of continuous learning and improvement. The skills you've honed here—whether in communication, leadership, or self-management—are foundational. They provide you with the tools to adapt, evolve, and thrive in an ever-changing world.

Application in Real Life

As you close this chapter of your learning journey, consider how you can apply these skills in your daily life:

- **Communication:** Practice active listening and clarity in your interactions.
- **Emotional Intelligence:** Understand your emotions and empathize with others.

- **Leadership:** Lead with integrity, inspire others, and foster collaboration.
- **Conflict Resolution:** Seek common ground and navigate disagreements constructively.
- **Self-Management:** Set goals, manage time effectively, and prioritize self-care.

Building Meaningful Connections

Life skills also enrich your relationships—both personal and professional. They enable you to build trust, communicate effectively, and resolve conflicts amicably. By investing in these skills, you cultivate deeper connections and create a positive impact on those around you.

Facing Challenges with Resilience

Inevitably, challenges will arise along your journey. Remember that resilience—fostered through these skills—empowers you to persevere in the face of adversity. Embrace setbacks as opportunities for growth and apply the problem-solving techniques you've learned to overcome obstacles.

Continuing Your Growth

Your journey towards mastering essential life skills does not end here. It is a lifelong pursuit fueled by curiosity, dedication, and a commitment to personal and professional development. Continue to seek new knowledge, challenge yourself, and refine your skills as you progress on your path.

Gratitude

Finally, I extend my heartfelt gratitude for accompanying me on this exploration of essential life skills. It has been a privilege to guide you through these pages, and I trust that the insights gained will serve you well on your journey forward.

Wishing you continued success, fulfillment, and growth as you apply these skills to create a life of purpose and impact.

www.ingramcontent.com/pod-product-compliance
Lightning Source LLC
Chambersburg PA
CBHW071953210526
45479CB00003B/921